TEACH YOUR CHILD TO FISH

Five Money Habits Every Child Should Master

WORKBOOK

Holly D. Reid, CPA

Dedication

A special thanks to my smart, creative, and talented sister, Toni, who brilliantly contributed to the development of the activities within this workbook.

Teach Your Child to Fish : Workbook
First Edition, March 2016

The Master Playbook
Atlanta, Georgia

Author	:	Holly D. Reid
Editor	:	Shayla Eaton, www.curiousediting.com
Cover Design	:	HappySelfPublishing.com
Graphic Design	:	Farkhanda M. Ishrat Shaikh

Scripture quotations marked (NLT) are taken from the Holy Bible, New Living Translation, copyright © 1996, 2004, 2007 by Tyndale House Foundation. Used by permission of Tyndale House Publishers, Inc., Carol Stream, Illinois 60188. All rights reserved.

The Authorized (King James) Version of the Bible ('the KJV'), the rights in which are vested in the Crown in the United Kingdom, is reproduced here by permission of the Crown's patentee, Cambridge University Press.

No part of this book may be reproduced in any written, electronic, recording, or photocopying without written permission of the publisher or author. The exception would be in the case of brief quotations embodied in the critical articles or reviews and pages where permission is specifically granted by the publisher or author.

Although every precaution has been taken to verify the accuracy of the information contained herein, the author assumes no responsibility for any errors or omissions. No liability is assumed for damages that may result from the use of information contained within.

Printed in the United States of America. All rights reserved.
© 2016

ISBN-13: 978-0-692-72003-5

"Give a man a fish and he will eat for a day. Teach a man to fish and he'll eat for a lifetime."
—Chinese Proverb

Teach Your Child to Fish supplemental workbook is a tool for parents to introduce their school-age children, kindergarten through high school, the five money-management habits discussed in the book. I encourage you to read *Teach Your Child to Fish* today by purchasing it on Amazon and to use this workbook to enhance your experience and to enforce the concepts within the book.

No one is born knowing how to fish. They must be taught and instructed. Similarly, once your child is taught the rules and given the tools for money management, they can be used for a lifetime.

Use the activities included to practice and reinforce building blocks for financial security as your child continues to grow, mature, and gain more exposure to money.

Say hello to a healthy financial future for your child as you incorporate these easy-to-implement activities into a daily or weekly routine with your kids.

WORKBOOK CONTENT

		PAGE NO.
Chapter One :	Work Hard and Be Rewarded	5
Chapter Two :	Spend Wisely and Consciously	11
Chapter Three :	Save First and Consistently	17
Chapter Four :	Use Credit Responsibly	21
Chapter Five :	Give Generously	25

CHAPTER ONE : WORK HARD AND BE REWARDED

ACTIVITY #1 : Household Chores

As we teach children about hard work, your first instinct may be to find chores in and around the house that they can do, and that's not a bad idea. In fact, this should be everyone's first experience in learning a good work ethic. The goal is to associate hard work with rewards.

Instructions : Visually track the task or chore to encourage accountability.

Example Tasks :

Pick up toys   Clean their room   Walk the dog   Prepare lunch for the family

Example Rewards :

Watch TV / Play video games 30 minutes   Dessert   New toy   Commission in increments from $0.25 to $5.00

Here is an example schedule to assign a chore to each child or member of the family.

Example : Household with 3 Children and a Pet

HOUSEHOLD CHORES

THE REID CHILDREN	SUNDAY	MONDAY	TUESDAY	WEDNESDAY	THURSDAY	FRIDAY	SATURDAY
LESLIE	Wash Dishes	Mop	Rake the Leaves	Rinse Fruits & Vegetables	Sort Laundry	Wipe Glass Doors	Set the Table
TONI	Rinse Dishes	Set the Table	Sweep the Driveway	Vacuum	Wash the Clothes	Vacuum	Empty the Trash
BRIDGET	Dry Dishes	Vacuum	Wash the Car	Set the Table	Fold the Clothes	Wash the Car	Empty the Recycling Bin

www.TheMasterPlaybook.com

HOUSEHOLD CHORES

Instructions : Write and assign a chore to each child or family member. Visually track the task or chore to encourage accountability.

YOUR FAMILY	SUNDAY	MONDAY	TUESDAY	WEDNESDAY	THURSDAY	FRIDAY	SATURDAY

www.TheMasterPlaybook.com

CHAPTER ONE : WORK HARD AND BE REWARDED

ACTIVITY #2 : Volunteer for a Cause

Instructions : Find a cause or charity that you or your child feels passionate about and make it a point to volunteer your time as a family. Consider a food or clothing bank, planting trees, delivering food to the disabled or elderly.

Cause or Charity : What cause or charity would you like to help with?

☐ Animals ☐ Bullying + Violence ☐ Disasters ☐ Discrimination ☐ Education

☐ Environment ☐ Health ☐ Homelessness + Poverty ☐ International

Time : How much do you have?   ☐ 1 hour or less   ☐ 2-5 hours   ☐ 5+ hours

Type : What would you like to do?

☐ Donate Something ☐ Make Something
☐ Work Face-to-Face ☐ Share Something
☐ Host an Event ☐ Start Something
☐ Improve a Space ☐ Take a Stand

Once an activity is selected and completed, discuss the following:

1. What activity did they enjoy most/least? And why?

_____

_____

2. How did their work help others?

_____

_____

3. What reward did they personally gain from sharing today?

_____

_____

www.TheMasterPlaybook.com

CHAPTER ONE : WORK HARD AND BE REWARDED

ACTIVITY #3: Name That Job

Instructions : In your everyday errands and routine, ask your child to name or identify at least three jobs being performed.

For example, during a visit to a grocery store, your child may notice the person stocking the shelves, the butcher at the meat counter, and the cashier adding the items being purchased.

Ask your child why the job is important and how are they helping people. This exercise can be done in almost any environment to raise awareness that everyone can work.

GROCERY STORE

Job Title	Importance of Job	How This Job Helps

LOCATION :

Job Title	Importance of Job	How This Job Helps

LOCATION :

Job Title	Importance of Job	How This Job Helps

CHAPTER ONE : WORK HARD AND BE REWARDED

ACTIVITY #4 : Commission Schedule

Pay your child for some chores : The rationale is there are some chores your child should do because they are deemed family responsibilities. As the parent, you can assign four to six chores that fall into the pay category with the understanding that the goal is to associate hard work with earning the reward of money.

Track each chore as it is completed on a daily basis : If the chore was not completed on that day, your child should not get paid. This presents the opportunity to teach honesty and ownership while encouraging repetition and consistency of daily tasks.

Reward your child immediately : Pay the earned commissions daily or weekly. This builds an immediate connection between the chores they did and the reward they received.

As an example, assign five commissionable chores worth $0.05 to $0.20 each. This gives your child the potential to earn $0.25 to $1.00 each day. Here is a snapshot of a commission schedule you can use for your child:

Daily Chores	Commission	MONDAY	TUESDAY
Make Bed	$ 0.05		
Food/Water for Dog	$ 0.05		
Set Table for Dinner	$ 0.05		
Put Away Clean Clothes	$ 0.05		
Extra Credit Chores	**Commission**		
Dust Furniture	$ 0.50		
Water Plants	$ 0.25		
Vacuum Living Room	$ 0.50		
Poor or Unacceptable Behavior	**Commission Reduction**		
Arguing with Parent or Siblings	-$ 0.25		
Disobedience	-$ 0.50		

Daily Chores : Select four to six chores that your child should be doing anyway and use the commission payment to encourage your child to establish a routine of completing these tasks every day. Value these chores lower than the next category.

Extra Credit Chores : Use this category to come up with tasks that perhaps you as a parent can remove from your to-do list. Increase the commission based on the degree of difficulty.

Unacceptable Behaviors : In the real world, there are rewards and consequences for the choices we make. Consider using the Commission Schedule as a way to discourage unacceptable behavior.

COMMISSION SCHEDULE

Here is a blank commission schedule you can use with your child:

	SUNDAY	MONDAY	TUESDAY	WEDNESDAY	THURSDAY	FRIDAY	SATURDAY
Chores							
Commission							
Poor or Unacceptable Behavior							
Commission Reduction							

CHAPTER TWO : SPEND WISELY AND CONSCIOUSLY

ACTIVITY #1A : Goal-Setting Session

Statistics show that people are far more likely to achieve written goals in comparison to those that are not written down. Habakkuk 2:2 (KJV) says, "And the LORD answered me, and said, Write the vision, and make it plain upon tables, that he may run that readeth it."

Money Goals

Instructions : Create three money goals to achieve in the next two to three weeks. Hang these goals on their bedroom wall, the refrigerator, or another public space in the home where they will see it every day.

Example money goals include :

I will save X amount by January 31st.
I will give X amount to {enter favorite charity, church, school} by December 1st.

1. _____
_____

2. _____
_____

3. _____
_____

Activity #1B : Vision Board

Instructions : If your child is more visual and creative by nature, consider creating a vision board together. Instead of writing their goals down in words, they can use images to depict their goals. They can create a digital vision board through offerings like PicStitch or Pinterest, or they can manually cut pictures from magazines or online images to create a physical vision board.

Materials Needed :

- ✓ Old Magazines
- ✓ Old Photographs
- ✓ Pens and Markers
- ✓ Scissors
- ✓ Glue
- ✓ Large Poster Board

After you've made a list of your goals and dreams in Activity #1A, start flipping through the magazines and photographs, cutting out images and words that relate to your goals and dreams. Once you've collected all the images and words you want to use, glue images and words cut from magazines or photographs, or drawn/written by hand, to a large piece of poster board however you like.

www.TheMasterPlaybook.com

CHAPTER TWO : SPEND WISELY AND CONSCIOUSLY

ACTIVITY #2 : Budgeting 101

A popular way to teach children about spending their money wisely is by sharing a very simple way to budget their spending using three categories :
Save, Spend, and Give.

Materials Needed :

- ✓ 3 Mason Jars or 3 Envelopes
- ✓ Pen, Markers, or Crayons
- ✓ Blank Paper or Images from Magazines
- ✓ Tape

Instructions : On either envelopes or jars, label each one SAVE, SPEND, GIVE. Have your child draw pictures or cut out images of what they plan to save their money for, spend their money on, or where they plan to give. Attach corresponding pictures to the jar or envelope.

Examples

ACTIVITY #3 : Plan Your Spending

Shop with a list and stick to it. This is an easy exercise that your child can help participate in any day of the week. You can make a list for back-to-school shopping, grocery shopping where they specifically write the items they would like to eat for breakfast or lunch, a school project, or for a sport they are participating in. Help them think through everything they may need and make a list that can come along on the shopping trip.

Shopping List :

1. _____
2. _____
3. _____
4. _____
5. _____

www.TheMasterPlaybook.com

CHAPTER TWO : SPEND WISELY AND CONSCIOUSLY

ACTIVITY #4 : Comparison Shop

Another great habit is to look for a great deal on the things needed. Check out sales and discount codes online for the store you plan to visit or specifically for the item you plan to purchase. If going to a grocery store or big retail store, have your child look up coupons for items on your list that they can either cut out, print out, or upload on an app for the store.

Example

	Price Comparison Worksheet			
Item	Store	New	Sales Price	Discount Code
Apple iPad	Apple	$ 169.99	$ 160.00	AB1CD5E
	Best Buy	$ 159.99	$ 150.00	F2GHI3J
	Target	$ 149.99	$ 140.00	KLMNO
	Walmart	$ 139.99	$ 130.00	PQRST

	Price Comparison Worksheet			
Item	Store	New	Sales Price	Discount Code

CHAPTER TWO : SPEND WISELY AND CONSCIOUSLY

ACTIVITY #5 : Distinguish between Needs vs. Wants

Here's a quick and practical exercise you can use to drive home your child's understanding and ability to distinguish between needs and wants.

Instructions : Call out different items in your home and ask your child to write them under the category Needs or Wants. Once you've called out about ten items, go back and discuss why they think the item should be placed in each category.

NEEDS	WANTS

CHAPTER TWO : SPEND WISELY AND CONSCIOUSLY

ACTIVITY #6 : Track Your Spending

Practice creating small budgets and make them more advanced as they get older. For younger children, start by creating a budget for a school project.

Instructions :
Make a shopping list before you go to the store using the template provided below.

Column 1 : Input an estimated amount you plan to spend next to each item listed.
Column 2 : Review your receipts and enter the amount you actually spent.
Column 3 : Calculate the difference between Estimated and Actual Cost.

Were you over, under, or right on target with your estimates?

SHOPPING LIST			
Item	Column 1 Estimated Cost	Column 2 Actual Cost	Column 3 Difference

ACTIVITY #7 : Create a Budget

For older children (ages thirteen and older), have your child create a budget for the school year. Create a budget one semester or one quarter at a time. Using the template below, they can begin creating a budget using broader spending categories like school clothes/uniforms, school supplies, class-specific projects, or social events like prom.

TRACK YOUR SPENDING MONTHLY			
Category	Budget Amount	Actual Amount	Difference
INCOME :			
Allowance/Commissions			
Wages/Income			
Monetary Donations			
INCOME SUBTOTAL			
EXPENSES :			
Snacks			
Outings			
Movies			
Clothing/School Uniform			
School Supplies			
Birthday Gifts			
Shopping			
Barber/Salon			
Miscellaneous/Other			
EXPENSES SUBTOTAL			
Net Income/(Loss)			

www.TheMasterPlaybook.com

CHAPTER THREE : SAVE FIRST AND SAVE CONSISTENTLY

ACTIVITY #1 : Save for a Rainy day

A portion of every home chore commission, monetary gift, or cash reward should be placed in a savings jar, piggy bank, or a savings account. Use this chart to record how much your child is saving. Keep it close to the savings jar or piggy bank.

MONEY SAVINGS CHART

Date	Allowance Earned	Amount Saved	Total in Bank

CHAPTER THREE : SAVE FIRST AND SAVE CONSISTENTLY

ACTIVITY #2 : Encourage Patience

When your child sets a savings goal, use a calendar to mark off each day they save. For example, tell your child to save for thirty days and mark each day they have waited. Consider adding incentives like matching their savings after they have saved for so many days. This exercise will encourage patience and delayed gratification on items they want to purchase.

| PATIENCE FOR SAVINGS CALENDAR |||||||
| JANUARY |||||||
SUNDAY	MONDAY	TUESDAY	WEDNESDAY	THURSDAY	FRIDAY	SATURDAY
					~~1~~	~~2~~
~~3~~	~~4~~	~~5~~	~~6~~	~~7~~	~~8~~	9
10	11	12	13	14	15	16
17	18	19	20	21	22	23
24	25	26	27	28	29	30
31						

My Goal for Saving This Month is $10
As an Incentive, My Parents Will Match My Savings after the Full 30 Days

| PATIENCE FOR SAVINGS CALENDAR |||||||
| MONTH : _____ |||||||
SUNDAY	MONDAY	TUESDAY	WEDNESDAY	THURSDAY	FRIDAY	SATURDAY

My Goal for Saving This Month is _____
As an Incentive, My Parents Will Match My Savings after _____

CHAPTER THREE : SAVE FIRST AND SAVE CONSISTENTLY

ACTIVITY #3 : Saving & Investing Word Search

Instructions : Complete this word search to enforce the concepts covered in Chapter 3 of the book.

Search these words ✓

- Save
- Savings Account
- Stock Certificate
- Certificate of Deposit
- Compound Interest
- Legacy
- Wealth
- Emergency Fund
- Self-Control
- Patience
- Invest
- Piggy Bank
- Retirement
- Dreams
- Dividends

www.TheMasterPlaybook.com

CHAPTER THREE : SAVE FIRST AND SAVE CONSISTENTLY

ACTIVITY #4 : Memory Verses

Instructions : For each Bible verse, fill in the blanks. Memorize and recite one verse per week. Challenge your child to find other Bible verses related to good money habits that they can learn.

1. Good _____ and hard _____ lead to prosperity, but hasty shortcuts lead to poverty. **Proverbs 21:5 (NLT)**

2. But divide your _____ among many places, for you do not know what _____ might lie ahead. **Ecclesiastes 11:2 (NLT)**

3. Just as the _____ rule the poor, so the borrower is _____ to the lender. **Proverbs 22:7 (NLT)**

4. The _____ have _____ and luxury, but _____ _____ whatever they get. **Proverbs 21:20 (NLT)**

5. Tell them to use their _____ to do good. They should be rich in _____ _____ and _____ to those in need, always being ready to _____ with others. **I Timothy 6:18 (NLT)**

CHAPTER FOUR : USE CREDIT RESPONSIBLY

ACTIVITY #1 : Brand Recognition

Instructions : Ask your child to write a brand name they are familiar with for each category listed below. Ask them how they know the brand's product that they listed. Use this exercise to have an open dialogue about marketing tactics used by businesses to encourage or influence you to purchase their services or products.

- Example: Fast Food Restaurant — McDonald's
- Car or Truck — _____
- Soap — _____
- Toothpaste — _____
- Lip Balm — _____
- Cellphone — _____
- Coffee — _____
- Cereal — _____
- Television Network — _____
- Petroleum Jelly — _____
- Body Lotion — _____
- Athletic Shoes — _____
- Potato Chips — _____
- Bottled Water — _____
- Pizza — _____
- Soda — _____
- Grocery Store — _____
- Jeans — _____

www.TheMasterPlaybook.com

CHAPTER FOUR : USE CREDIT RESPONSIBLY

ACTIVITY #2 : Family IOU

Instructions : Using the IOU below, create an IOU (I Owe You) in the family for a week. For the next seven days, take on each other's chores or loan one another money. After week one is over, have an open dialogue about how it felt to owe someone else.

IOU NOTE

I _____Kimberly M._____ hereby declare that I owe _____Alfred M._____ the amount of _____$200_____, borrowed on _____4th March 2016_____ to be paid in full

By : _____4th April 2016_____

Full name _____Kimberly M._____ Signature _____Kimberly M._____

Lender's name _____Alfred M._____ Signature _____Alfred M._____

Witnessed by _____Ebony S._____ Signature _____ES_____

IOU NOTE

I _____ hereby declare that I owe _____ the amount of _____, borrowed on _____ to be paid in full

By : _____

Full name _____ Signature _____

Lender's name _____ Signature _____

Witnessed by _____ Signature _____

How did it feel to owe someone something?

_____

_____

I OWE YOU

What if you were not able to repay, what should happen? Explain.

_____

_____

_____

www.TheMasterPlaybook.com

CHAPTER FOUR : USE CREDIT RESPONSIBLY

ACTIVITY #3 : Use Credit Responsibly Word Search

Instructions: Complete this word search and find the words and concepts discussed in Chapter 4 of the book.

A	J	S	D	N	S	A	V	A	L	U	E	A	C	C	V	U	N	S	S
S	G	O	O	D	D	E	B	T	X	B	O	R	R	O	W	E	R	C	P
Y	R	O	K	U	F	P	L	B	A	D	D	E	B	T	L	A	E	H	E
R	C	R	E	D	I	T	O	R	J	V	Y	K	P	M	D	S	B	O	N
A	P	P	R	E	C	I	A	T	I	N	G	A	S	S	E	T	S	L	D
F	D	P	A	I	D	I	N	F	U	L	L	T	U	R	B	O	X	A	W
E	R	E	T	I	R	E	S	E	N	T	C	L	N	G	T	G	P	R	I
M	A	R	K	E	T	I	N	G	T	R	A	P	S	E	F	O	S	S	S
G	A	T	U	P	W	O	C	R	E	D	I	T	C	A	R	D	A	H	E
N	P	R	E	P	A	I	D	C	A	R	D	J	N	C	E	U	V	I	L
Q	S	F	I	N	A	N	C	E	C	H	A	R	G	E	E	M	E	P	Y
A	E	I	O	U	Z	K	F	P	B	R	O	R	D	C	W	F	L	S	T

Search these words

- [ ] Borrower
- [ ] Creditor
- [ ] Debt-Free
- [ ] Finance Charge
- [ ] Spend Wisely
- [ ] Paid in Full
- [ ] Credit Card
- [ ] Prepaid Card
- [ ] Marketing Traps
- [ ] Appreciating Assets
- [ ] Value
- [ ] Scholarships
- [ ] Loans
- [ ] Bad Debt
- [ ] Good Debt

www.TheMasterPlaybook.com

CHAPTER FOUR : USE CREDIT RESPONSIBLY

ACTIVITY #4 : Ten Commandments of Financial Stewardship

We are called to be stewards of the resources we have been given. As your child begins their journey with money, review and print this compilation as a reminder to make wise decisions and to practice the five money-management habits addressed in *Teach Your Child to Fish*.

I
Work hard and with integrity.

II
Live within 80% of your means.

III
Tithe 10% of your time, talents, and treasures.

IV
Save 10% of your gross pay.

V
Pay off consumer debt as fast as you can.

VI
Set 1 or 2 challenging financial goals annually, and COMPLETE them.

VII
Identify & connect with an Accountability Partner to stay on track.

VIII
Pray to God, praise him, and share your testimony of financial success with others.

IX
Give to others and support a cause you believe in.

X
Invest wisely and leave a solid, financial legacy for others to build upon.

www.TheMasterPlaybook.com

CHAPTER FIVE : GIVE GENEROUSLY

Activity #1 : Teach Your Child to Tithe

Materials Needed :

✓ Plain envelope   ✓ Bible   ✓ Pen/Pencil/Markers

Instructions :

1

Encourage your child to find a scripture about giving or tithing and have them read it aloud. Here is one to start: II Corinthians 9:7.

2

Write their name, date, scripture, and amount of their tithe on the front of the envelope.

3

Have them draw pictures on the back of the envelope showing how they earned the money they are giving or donating.

4

Take the envelope to church and allow them to deliver their offering.

www.TheMasterPlaybook.com

CHAPTER FIVE : GIVE GENEROUSLY

Activity #2 : Charity Box

Instructions : Mark a container in your home that can be routinely filled with gently used clothing and toys to donate to those less fortunate. The clothes and toys can be things that the family has outgrown or are no longer used or needed. Make a trip to a charity that needs it and personally deliver the items.

www.TheMasterPlaybook.com

CHAPTER FIVE : GIVE GENEROUSLY

Activity #3 : Care Packages for the Homeless

Instructions : Assemble care packages that can be personally delivered to a homeless shelter or kept in the car and shared in a spontaneous opportunity.

Place 6 to 8 items into a sandwich or quart-sized Ziploc bag and keep them out of direct sunlight.

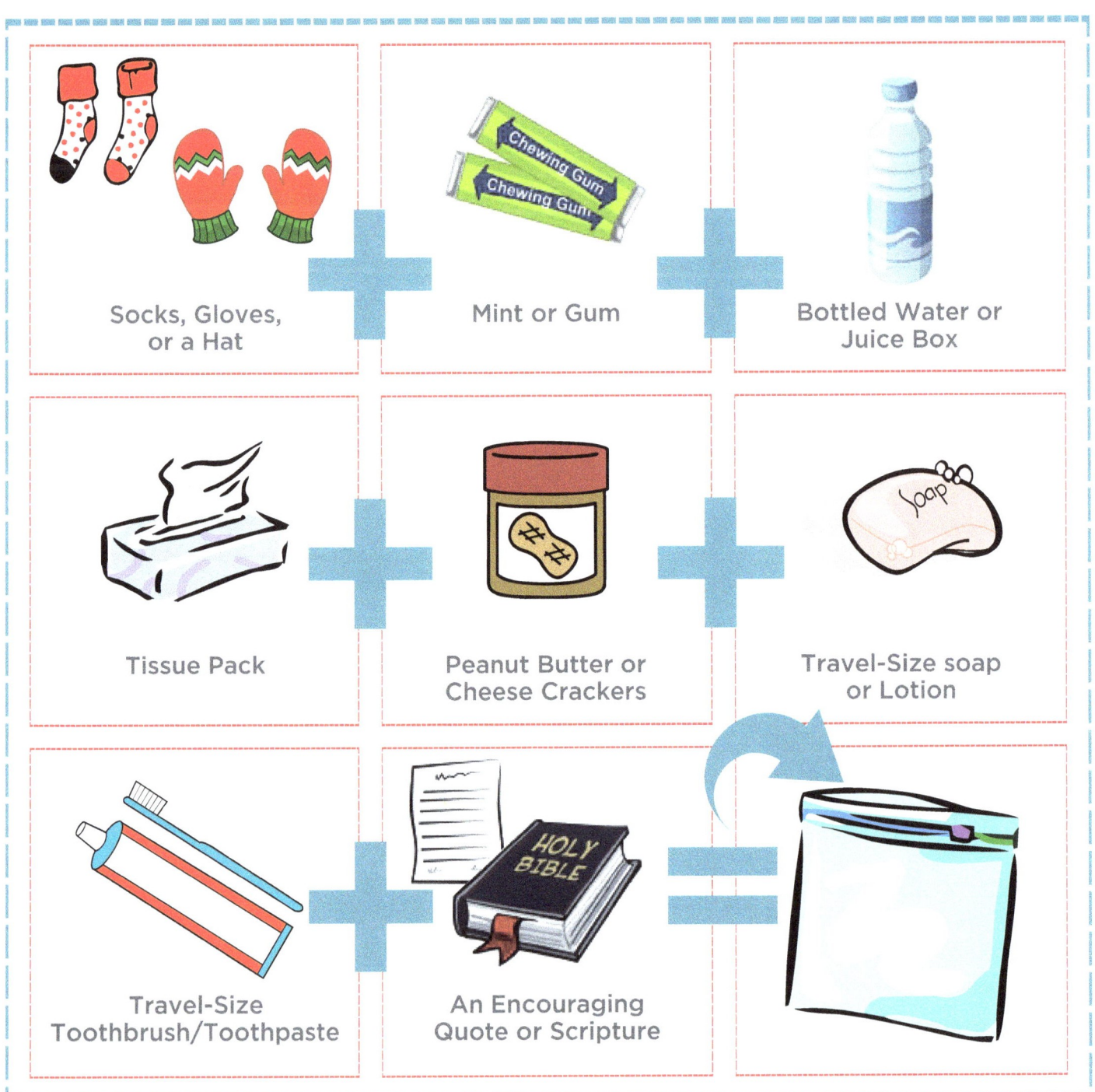

Socks, Gloves, or a Hat + Mint or Gum + Bottled Water or Juice Box

Tissue Pack + Peanut Butter or Cheese Crackers + Travel-Size soap or Lotion

Travel-Size Toothbrush/Toothpaste + An Encouraging Quote or Scripture =

www.TheMasterPlaybook.com

Activity #4 : Make Giving a Part of Your Spending Plan

Instructions : Giving should come from the heart. Ask your child how they would like to help others.

How I Plan to Help Others

MONTH	TIME AND TALENT	TREASURE	PLACE TO DONATE

www.TheMasterPlaybook.com

CHAPTER FIVE : GIVE GENEROUSLY

ACTIVITY #5 : Money Habits Word Search

Instructions : Complete this word search to help your child learn and remember the words and concepts discussed in Chapter 5.

M	G	I	A	C	C	O	U	N	T	A	B	L	E	T
K	O	Q	X	I	D	D	O	N	A	T	I	O	N	R
A	O	C	R	H	A	R	D	W	O	R	K	N	T	E
B	D	O	J	V	Y	R	P	M	V	T	B	F	R	A
E	S	M	G	I	T	E	S	E	T	I	T	H	E	S
G	T	M	S	A	A	W	E	R	F	M	X	U	P	U
E	E	I	N	S	L	A	R	G	R	E	P	Y	R	R
N	W	S	T	S	E	R	V	E	U	O	S	I	E	E
E	A	S	P	E	N	D	I	N	G	P	L	A	N	B
R	R	I	F	T	T	J	C	C	A	U	V	G	E	K
O	D	O	M	S	Q	A	E	Y	L	M	E	I	U	O
U	N	N	S	L	H	G	I	F	T	D	N	V	R	L
S	G	O	A	L	S	E	T	T	I	N	G	E	C	F
I	N	F	P	J	D	P	V	P	U	R	P	O	S	E

Search these words ✓

- ☐ Goal-Setting
- ☐ Frugal
- ☐ Hard Work
- ☐ Good Steward
- ☐ Commission
- ☐ Reward
- ☐ Service
- ☐ Donation
- ☐ Tithe
- ☐ Give
- ☐ Accountable
- ☐ Be Generous
- ☐ Gift
- ☐ Spending Plan
- ☐ Assets
- ☐ Time
- ☐ Talent
- ☐ Treasure
- ☐ Entrepreneur
- ☐ Purpose

www.TheMasterPlaybook.com

CONGRATULATIONS!

Well done for reaching the end of the workbook!

If you have reached this point, your child has been introduced to the five money-management habits every child should master. Continue to practice and reinforce these lessons as they grow, mature, and take on more responsibility.

Did you enjoy the activities in this workbook? If so, chances are someone you know will too. Please share your experience with others and continue to spread the word.

I would also like to hear your feedback and any insights you'd like to share. Please leave your review on Amazon or Goodreads. Sign up for more information at www.TheMasterPlaybook.com and follow me on social media.

 TheMasterPlaybook

 @TheMasterPlaybook

 @MasterPlaybook

ABOUT THE BOOK

Don't you wish someone would've taken the time to teach you money-management concepts at a young age? Think for a moment what your life would be like. How important would that be to share with your child or grandchild?

The unfortunate reality is the absence of financial literacy at home and in our schools creates a society filled with victims of the consumer culture, bound in debt, and working well beyond retirement age – not because they want to, but because they to. Today's youth face a future of similar obstacles because they are learning sound financial concepts and practicing ideal money-management habits too late in life.

This easy-to-digest playbook provides guiding principles and practical activities to teach school-age children, kindergarten through high school, money management concepts they should adopt as they begin to understand money. Each activity is designed to enforce a key money habit and are easy and fun to implement.

Teach Your Child to Fish **will give you the tools to:**

- Guide your child to discover the work they are called to do and feed their **entrepreneurial spirit.**

- Expose marketing traps and provide **proven strategies** to avoid debt, make conscious spending decisions and maneuver through common financial pitfalls.

- Use scripture and **biblical references** to support and reinforce healthy money habits.

- Fill the **financial literacy gap** where school systems fail to teach kids about money.

- Provide the building blocks for your child to begin **saving and investing** for their future.

- Introduce the three T's of Giving by using their **Treasure, Time, and Talent.**

Follow the advice and complete the recommended activities in this book and notice how quickly your child begins to echo what they've learned.

Purchase the book today on Amazon.

ABOUT THE AUTHOR

As a personal finance advocate, Holly Reid is on a mission to motivate, inspire, and help others manage their finances as responsible stewards. Holly's philosophy is grounded in the basic principles of living debt-free, saving for the future, and investing wisely. She believes each person has the power to create a healthy financial future.

She is a Certified Public Accountant and finance professional with over 15 years of experience serving the media and entertainment industry. She currently offers her expertise through interactive sessions designed to educate and inform groups on how to apply financial principles and promote financial literacy to teenagers and young adults.

As the youngest of four siblings, Holly is no stranger of doing more with less. Exposure to the broad economic landscape, and its disparities, piqued her interest to understand money management and propelled her to discover savvy ways to save and experience financial harmony as an adult. Furthermore, her personal financial mistakes and rebounds now fuel her to build a legacy worth leaving.